# OLD RIVINGTON & DISTRICT

by

## M. D. Smith
### In collaboration with E. M. Brownlow

## Wyre Publishing

**North Villas, Garstang Road, St. Michael's on Wyre, Lancashire, PR3 OTE**

ISBN 0 9526187 1 0

Jack and Lena Taylor photographed
outside St. Paul's Church, Adlington.

# CONTENTS

# ACKNOWLEDGEMENTS

My first duty is to record sincere thanks to Martin Brownlow who has worked with me on the completion of this project and to my wife Andrea, for many hours spent typing and checking the manuscript.

The undermentioned have provided valuable assistance in varying degrees and I am pleased to acknowledge their kindness.

| | |
|---|---|
| Fred Ashworth | Pall Mall Cottages, Rivington |
| Edward Brownlow | Brownlow Road, Horwich |
| Joan Birchall | Foxholes, Horwich |
| Willoughby Burgess | Babylon Lane, Adlington |
| Albert Clayton | St. Michael's on Wyre |
| Derek Coupe | Stock's Park, Horwich |
| Kathleen Crompton | Hazlemere, Surrey |
| Roger Crompton | Rivington Farm, Surrey |
| Geoffrey Drinkwater | Lever Park Avenue, Horwich |
| Sybil Hart | Dufton, Appleby, Cumbria |
| Ian and Sue Harper | Pennine Road, Horwich |
| Brenda Haworth | Stock's Park, Horwich |
| Dorothy Kershaw | Major Bottoms, Anderton |
| Mrs. N. Makinson | Pall Mall Cottages, Rivington |
| Anne Middleton | Belmont View, Bolton |
| David Owen | Chorley Road, Westhoughton |
| Rosemary Robinson | Scarborough, Yorkshire |
| Rhoda Salmon | Rivington Hall, Rivington |
| Alice and James Winstanley | Babylon Lane, Adlington |
| Bolton Evening News | |

## SPECIAL ACKNOWLEDGEMENT

Much of the historical detail contained in this work has been gleaned from earlier publications including the 'History of Horwich' by Thomas Hampson (1893); 'A Short History of the Township of Rivington' by William Fergusson Irvine (1904); and 'About Rivington' by John Rawlinson (1969).

In addition to his book, John Rawlinson made copious notes on the history of the locality which I have found to be of much benefit. As a special acknowledgement I have included a personal photograph of John and his wife Agnes, to serve as a memorial.

John and Agnes Rawlinson of Crown Lane, Horwich.

**Aerial view of Rivington. c.1950:** The village green is to the right of centre with Rivington Church far left.

# INTRODUCTION

Set amid hills and man-made lakes, the village of Rivington has managed to retain much of the idyllic charm and pastoral peace of a bygone age. There are still places in the area where one can enjoy solitude even when thousands of visitors are in attendance. A walk towards the reservoirs or upwards to the Pike Tower, Winter Hill or Lead Mines Clough soon distances one from the more sedentary visitor who prefers to enjoy the surroundings from a vehicle parked close to the amenities at the two 'barns', or on one of the car parks sited at vantage points to afford panoramic views.

Rivington was always a popular spot to visit even before the motor car became so prevalent and within the financial reach of so many people. However, in those days the frequency of trips out was proportionately less due to a combination of long working hours and poverty which curtailed the opportunity for leisure pursuits and visitors were of necessity from a more local catchment area. This meant that there were long periods when the residents were left in peace with only the birds and wild animals to break the tranquillity.

The popularity of Rivington is evinced to some degree in the number of old post-card views which exist of the village and its environs. Several local photographers, including Ralph Close & Son of Horwich; Claude Cross of Horwich; W. J. Sandiford of Chorley; Luke Berry of Chorley and A. J. Evans, Ltd., of Preston, took views in and around Rivington about the turn of the century and these form an important contemporary pictorial record.

Martin Brownlow with whom I have collaborated to produce this work has had an interest in Rivington and its history since he was a child and has managed to amass an excellent collection of photographs and documents relating to the village. My own interest stems from researches into the publication of 'Leverhulme's Rivington' (1984) which is the story of the Rivington Bungalow. A selection from our joint collections augmented by material from various other sources and including some previously unpublished photographs forms the basis of this book. It is hoped that the contents will both give pleasure and provoke nostalgia.

It seems appropriate as the twenty first century approaches to record how Rivington once appeared if only to reinforce the need to preserve our heritage and retain as far as possible such a lovely unspoiled spot for future generations to enjoy.

Malcolm David Smith,
Adlington, Lancashire.
July 1995

# RIVINGTON – Historical Notes

There is evidence of Bronze Age settlement in and around Rivington in the shape of the Winter Hill and Noon Hill Tumuli on Rivington Moor and the Pike Stones Megalithic Tomb and Round Loaf Saucer Tumulus on Anglezarke Moor. In addition, 'Coblowe' on the banks of the Lower Rivington Reservoir, where Lord Leverhulme had a replica of the ruins of Liverpool Castle built in the 1920's, may also have been an ancient burial ground because the word 'low' when used in connection with place names almost invariably identifies such a site.

Rivington could well be one of Lancashire's 'ington' settlements dating from around 650 A.D. However, the first written reference to Rivington appears in 1202 in a plea of assize for Mort d'ancestor in which Alexander Pilkington is referred to as the Lord of Rivington Manor.

The Pilkington family has long connections with Rivington down the centuries, Richard Pilkington is credited as being the founder of Rivington Church which was built in 1540 and Bishop James Pilkington - the first Protestant Bishop over the Catholic See of Durham - founded Rivington Grammar School in 1566. The last surviving issue of this noble family was Robert Pilkington who died in 1605. By his will dated 16th November 1605, Robert Pilkington left his estate in trust to Mr. Serjeant Hutton, Mr. Thomas Tildsley and Mrs Catherine Pilkington who eventually sold the property to Robert Lever of D'arcy Lever and Thomas Breres of Preston.

In 1729 the Breres family sold out their interest in Rivington Manor to John Andrews. In 1733 John Andrews had the tower built on Rivington Pike. It was erected during an important court case which had the effect of properly establishing the boundary between Rivington and Horwich. Robert Andrews succeeded to the Rivington Estate in 1765 as great nephew and heir-in-law to John Andrews. Robert had Rivington Hall partially demolished and replaced with the red brick building that is so familiar today. Lucy Andrews married Woodhouse Crompton of Liverpool in 1834 and their eldest son, John William Crompton came into possession of the estate in 1865.

William Hesketh Lever (later Lord Leverhulme)

eventually purchased Rivington Manor from the Crompton family in 1900.

Generally speaking the main reservoir system at Rivington comprising High Bullough Reservoir, the Upper and Lower Rivington Reservoirs, Anglezarke Reservoir, Rake or Red Bank Reservoir, Lower Roddlesworth Reservoir and the filter beds at the southern end of the Lower Rivington Reservoir, was constructed in the years 1850 to 1857 inclusive. Increased demand for water in Liverpool resulted in the addition of the Upper Roddlesworth Reservoir in 1865 and the Yarrow Reservoir in 1875.

Lord Leverhulme's influence resulted in the construction of the Bungalow and grounds and the gift of Lever Park. These issues are dealt with separately because they amount to the greatest change that has taken place in the area since the construction of the reservoirs.

Wages list for Rivington Manor compiled for John Andrews - dated 8th May 1736.

**View of Rivington Pike from George's Lane, Horwich. c.1910:** George's Lane was much improved during Lord Leverhulme's time to afford access to the Bungalow which stood on the 1,000 foot contour of Rivington Moor just below the Pike Tower. The building to the left of centre is Higher Meadows Farm and the one far left, near the skyline, is Prospect Farm.

**Rivington Lane viewed from the Lower Rivington Reservoir. c.1920:** Pall Mall Cottages are to the right with Beech Cottage in the centre and Beech House on the left.

**Rivington Village. c.1905:** This photograph of Rivington Village was taken from the meadow beside the church. The vicarage is to the right with the terrace of properties beside the village green in the centre. Far left can be seen the cupola on the roof of Rivington Chapel.

**Rivington Village Green. c.1920:** A number of disputes have arisen over the years concerning the access to Rivington Chapel from the village green. The wall to the chapel is visible extreme left and it is the width of the access drive which has caused concern. One argument put forward was that dancing was always staged on the green on the annual club days and if too much width was afforded to the chapel driveway this would be prevented. The counter argument was that there should be sufficient room to allow a carriage and four horses to complete a turn at the end of the driveway. Fortunately the dispute has long since been amicably resolved. Rivington Post Office is the property to the left.

*Above:* **Black - A - Moor's Head Hotel. c.1900:** A pub of the same name stood on a nearby site until the reservoirs were built in the 1850's and it was demolished to lie under the waters of the Upper Rivington Reservoir. The Inn sign, a stone carving of a Moor's head, was built into the wall of nearby New Hall Farm barn. The second pub (shown above) was the centre of much village life particularly celebrations. The pub was demolished in 1903 but the bowling green was retained and is presently used by Rivington Village Club which was built close by.

Mrs Ann Gerrard was born in 1816 and at the time that this photograph was taken she was the landlady of the Black - A - Moor's Head Hotel. (c.1890) She died in 1907.

# Rivington Hall

RIVINGTON HALL LEVER PARK.

**Rivington Hall. c.1905:** Originally constructed in 1485, Rivington Hall was a timbered dwelling which was eventually partially demolished by Robert Andrews, Lord of Rivington Manor, in 1774, and replaced by the existing structure. Date stones at the rear of the Hall include the dates 1694 and 1700 which suggest alterations / additions to the building.

**Rear of Rivington Hall. c.1910:** The Mulligan family can be seen at the back of the Hall. Alterations to the back of the Hall were carried out between 1694 and 1700.

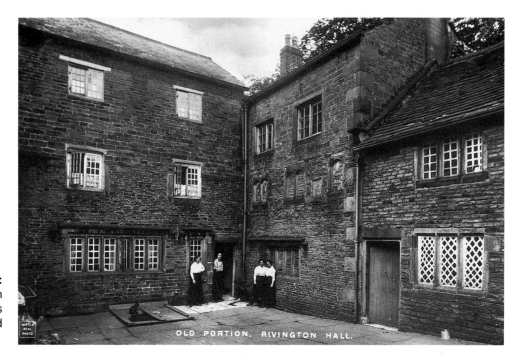

OLD PORTION. RIVINGTON HALL.

*Above:* **Rivington Hall. c.1911:** The Mulligan family held the franchise from Lord Leverhulme to supply refreshments for visitors to the upper and lower barns at Rivington. John Mulligan is seated with his wife standing immediate right and their five daughters.

*Right:* Thomas Milner who owned the Bridgefoot Smithy in Horwich photographed behind Rivington Hall by Mrs Kathleen Crompton in 1948. The datestone over the door relates to William Breres who carried out alterations / additions to the Hall in 1694.

# Lords of Rivington Manor

**Robert Andrews of Rivington Hall. c.1852:** Robert Andrews was born on 13th January 1785 and inherited Rivington Manor on the death of his parents. His mother died on the 29th April 1791 and his father on the 13th August 1793. He remained single and enjoyed considerable local standing as a Justice of the Peace and Deputy Lieutenant of Lancashire. He died on the 4th July 1858 when the estate passed to his younger brother, John Andrews.

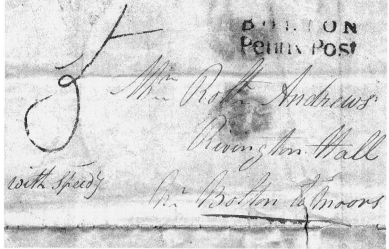

*Below and right:* Letter from John Bury of Whalley to Robert Andrews, of Rivington Hall. 5th June 1822.

Sir

I purpose to meet you at Bolton the next Monday June 10th at Eleven o'clock in the forenoon at the Bridge Inn — When you will I hope have the deeds ready for delivery

Whalley
June 5th 1822

I am Sir
your obt. Servant
John Bury

**John William Crompton of Rivington Hall. c.1890:** John William Crompton inherited Rivington Estate on the death of his uncle, John Andrews, in 1865. He eventually sold the estate to Lord Leverhulme in 1900.

**Andrews Crompton of Rivington Hall. c.1900:** John William Crompton and his wife, Margaret, had two sons - Andrews and Theodore Crompton. Andrews Crompton and his family lived at Rivington Hall.

**Shooting Lodge, Anglezarke. c.1900:** The shooting lodge pictured above was situated on the moorland above Lead Mines Clough. Andrews Crompton is to the left of the party with Cecil Winders, a Bolton solicitor, coat-less, to the right and in front of him.

Mrs Andrews Crompton holding her son, John William Richardson Crompton who was born in July 1908. The photograph was taken beside Rivington Hall. Mrs Crompton's maiden name was MOSS and she was the daughter of a mill-owner from Bolton.

John William Richardson Crompton as a young man. He was the last of the Crompton descent to be born at Rivington Hall.

# Rivington Pike

John Andrews who owned half of Rivington Moor in 1729 bought the other half from John Breres that year for £1,747. At this time the manor consisted of the Hall, a number of occupied farms and the common or waste lands on the hillside. The latter amounted to 400 acres.

The tenants of the manor had certain rights of turbary (cutting peat for fuel) and pasturage (the right to graze cattle) written into their leases and these rights were a constant source of friction. The main reason was that the boundaries of moor common were uncertain and often disregarded.

On the 7th March 1733 two employees of John Andrews seized a cow belonging to Christopher Horrocks of Horwich, on the grounds that the cow was grazing on land owned by John Andrews. Protracted litigation ensued which was eventually resolved in 1737 in favour of John Andrews although at considerable cost. Nevertheless the court case resulted in the boundary between Rivington and Horwich being properly drawn.

The Tower on Rivington Pike was erected by John Andrews ostensibly to celebrate the acquisition of Rivington Manor in 1729 but it could also be argued that he erected the structure as evidence of legal ownership of the moor.

At the time of the Spanish Armada in 1588 there is mention of the Beacon on Rivington Pike. If the Armada was sighted off Plymouth Sound a chain of beacons stretching the length and breadth of the country was to be lit to warn the populace.

Rivington Pike Tower was constructed of some of the stone from the earlier beacon and the sharp grit boulders of the hillside along with stone from the Douglas Stream. The tower is 20 feet high with the external walls forming a square each side being 17 feet long. It was a single storey building with a cellar and was roofed. The inner chamber, measuring 13 feet square, was heated with a fireplace.

Over the years the Pike Tower fell into disrepair and at one stage plans were mooted to demolish the structure because it was dangerous. Fortunately the decision was taken to restore the building and it now receives regular upkeep and maintenance.

**Rivington Pike Tower. c.1880:** Photographer Luke Berry of the Excelsior Studio, Chorley, issued this old cabinet photograph of the Pike Tower. Seated in front of the tower are Mrs Margaret Evelyn Crompton with her two sons - Andrews and Theodore. John William Crompton, the boys' father, is standing in the centre of the group to the left.

**Rivington Pike. c.1900:** Rivington Church spire can be seen in the centre of the photograph with the Black - A - Moor's Head Inn to the right and Rivington Vicarage to the left. The Pike Tower stands on the horizon.

**Rivington Hill and Pike Tower, 1915:** The reverse of this postcard reads, "Date on tablet in front of tower 1733. Height of hill 1498' above sea level. Card from Sister Lucy - April 30 1915".

WATER TOWER, RIVINGTON PIKE.

Pike Tower. c.1920.

# Rivington Church and Vicarage

**Rivington Church. c.1875:** Rivington Church was built in 1540 and consecrated by Doctor Bird, Bishop of Chester, on the 11th October 1541. The church was built on the site of a former place of worship to which references exist as early as the thirteenth century.

Rivington Church, c.1900.

**Rivington Church. c.1880:** A bell house which was built in 1540 to accommodate a bell can be seen on the north side of the church; although one was purchased in 1542 it was never hung for use. The structure has been used as a charnel house and sexton's house over the years.

*Below:* The left hand photograph shows the charnel house, whilst the right hand photograph shows gravestones around the south entrance porch of the ivy covered Rivington Church. c.1880.

*Above:* **Entrance to Rivington Church. c.1920:** A lych gate was erected at the entrance in 1923 in memory of the Reverend William Ritson. M.A., who was the vicar of Rivington from 1879 to 1918.

*Below:* Interior of Rivington Church photographed by Claude Cross of Horwich, c.1920.

**Fisher House, Rivington. c.1890:** Reverend J. Fisher, who was the incumbent at Rivington Church from 1763 until 1813, lived at Fisher House for a period during 1774. At the time of this photograph the premises were in use as a Temperance Hotel.

**Rivington Vicarage. c.1875:** The first purpose built accommodation for the incumbent at Rivington Church was provided in 1834. This was eventually demolished and replaced with a second building in 1884.

**Rivington Village Green with Rivington Vicarage to the right. c.1905:** Reverend Ritson who was vicar of Rivington Church from 1879 until 1918 paid half the cost of a new vicarage which was completed in 1884 and built on the same site as the original vicarage. The remainder was met with capital from the church authorities.

Close up view of the rear of Rivington Vicarage. c.1900.

Reverend William Ritson. M.A., who was vicar of Rivington from 1879 to 1918 can be seen with his family taking tea on the vicarage lawn. The lady on the extreme left is Miss Mary Susan Ainsworth of Beech House, Rivington.

Reverend G. E. Owen, Vicar of Rivington, walking in the area with Johnny Miller of Chapel House, Rivington, about 1952.

Harry King of Long Lane, Heath Charnock, who was the organist at Rivington Church from 1929 until 1969. He followed Matthew Makinson and was, in turn, followed by David Cunliffe, Mrs Eileen Jermy and Martin Brownlow.

# Rivington Chapel

**Rivington Chapel. c.1905:** John Andrews of Rivington sold the land on which Rivington Chapel was built for £2. 10s. 0d, plus an annual rental fee of twopence to be paid at the Feast of St. John the Baptist. The chapel was opened for worship on the 10th June 1703. John Walker was the first minister but he died in 1702 before the chapel was consecrated for worship. He was succeeded by Reverend Ralph Ainsworth.

**Rivington Chapel Interior. 1903:** The Willoughby Monument is to the left of centre near to the pulpit. The old box-type pews are still in use at the chapel.

**Frances Hibbert (nee Andrews) c.1795:** This copy of a portrait held in a locket is of Frances Hibbert (nee Andrews) who was the wife of Nathaniel Hibbert, Minister at Rivington Chapel. Frances was the cousin of Robert Andrews of Rivington Hall. She died on the 10th April 1830, aged 68 years.

29 November'/80.

Rivington,

PER POST. Nr Chorley,

Lancashire,

PER RAIL Adlington.

My dear Sir.    Rivington Chapel.

At a meeting of the congregation held yesterday afternoon, it was unanimously resolved that you be invited to take the pastorate as soon as convenient Say from 1st of January next, & it was thought desirable that if possible you should supply in December after the first Sunday, when Mr Mason takes the services. I am very truly yours

J.W.C.

Red Samt Thompson

Copy of a letter from John William Crompton of Rivington Hall inviting Samuel Thompson to accept the incumbency of Rivington Chapel. Dated 29th November 1880.

2 Carnarvon St
Queen's Road
Manchester 1st Dec 1880.

My dear Sir,

It is with much pleasure that I have just received your letter conveying the unanimous invitation of a Meeting of the Rivington Congregation to myself, to become their Minister.

I accept the invitation most heartily, and shall, in accordance with the expressed wish of the Meeting, enter upon the duties of the Pastorate in the beginning of next year. (1st Jany 1881.)

I shall also supply for the three last Sundays in December as requested.

With many th the kind invitation I have received, I Am
My dear Sir
Yours most truly
Sam Thompson

**Rivington Chapel entrance. c.1910:** Reverend Samuel Thompson, who was the Minister of Rivington Chapel from 1881 to 1918, is standing outside the chapel entrance pictured with members of the Winstanley family.

**Chapel House, Rivington. 24th April, 1963:** Chapel House was built in 1786 for the incumbent at Rivington Chapel. Interestingly, the property contained an integral stable and there is a small water trough opposite the house. At the time that the photograph was taken, Mr James Murray (pictured), a plumber of Church Street, Horwich, was carrying out work at the property.

Miss Dorothy Kershaw (left) and Mrs. Florence Woosey photographed outside Rivington Chapel. Both women have a long association with chapel business. Mrs Woosey was a trustee for many years and sadly died in 1989. Miss Kershaw still retains her trusteeship despite failing health. Her knowledge of the chapel and its history has been of invaluable service in solving disputes over the years.

## Rivington Chapel.

A

# Lantern Lecture

WILL BE GIVEN BY

### Rev. W. T. BUSHROD, of Chorley,

ON

### Thursday, Feb. 8th, 1923.

SUBJECT:

## "THROUGH FRANCE,"

FROM SEA TO SEA

### PARIS, SERVES, ROUEN, LYONS,

WITH VIEWS OF

*Cathedrals. Street Scenes, National Monuments, etc.*

Chair to be taken at 7-30 p.m. by

## GEO. N. SHAWCROSS, Esq.

Lanternist — THOS. ARCHER, Esq.

### ALL WELCOME.     COLLECTION.

*Printed by FLETCHERS', Longworth Road, Horwich,*

Handbill for a 'Magic' Lantern show at Rivington Chapel - 8th February 1923.

# Rivington Grammar School

The original Rivington Grammar School was founded by Bishop James Pilkington in 1566 under a charter granted by Queen Elizabeth I. The school was completely re-built in 1714. The building shown above is the first Rivington Grammar School, but when Rivington and Blackrod Grammar Schools combined in 1873 a completely new school building was erected approximately two miles away, which was officially opened on the 23rd January 1882. The above photograph dates from 1875.

**Rivington and Blackrod Grammar School. c.1900:** Blackrod Grammar School, founded in 1568 by John Holmes, citizen and weaver of London; amalgamated with Rivington Grammar School in 1873 and an entirely new building was provided for the united schools. The old Rivington Grammar School building was taken into use as a day school while Blackrod Grammar School was handed over to the township for educational purposes.

**Rivington and Blackrod Grammar School. c.1900.** A group of children can be seen at the entrance to the school. The young girl in front of the group is holding tethers to a donkey and a dog.

Request for donations to mark the retirement of Mr and Mrs Archer, headmaster and headmistress of Rivington School after 32 years service.

Rivington School.

RIVINGTON,

DEAR SIR,                    JUNE, 1924.

Mr. and Mrs. ARCHER are retiring from their duties as Headmaster and Headmistress after a service of 32 years.

A Committee of Past and Present Pupils and Residents of the District, has been formed to mark the occasion by a suitable PRESENTATION in recognition of Mr. and Mrs. Archer's devoted service at the School and in the Parish, and this will take place in the School on Saturday, July 5th, at 3-30 p.m.

The Committee hope they may include your name in the list of Subscribers, and also have your support at the Presentation, at which Lord Leverhulme will preside.

Subscriptions may be sent to any of the Committee, if possible before June 23rd, to enable the arrangements to be completed.

Yours truly,

Ernest Ashton, Chorley
E. J. Bonnor, Rivington
John King, Adlington
Rev. H. E. Lovelady,
        Rivington
R. Ratcliffe, Rivington
John Miller, Rivington
John Mulligan, Rivington
W. Smith, Rivington
Jones

A. Smith, Anderton
Miss A. Ratcliffe,
        Rivington
Miss Hodson, Chorley
Mrs. A. Harding,
        Heath Charnock
Mrs. J. Howarth,
        Heath Charnock

G. N. Shawcross, Chairman.

**Rivington Day School. c.1900:** This was the original grammar school - an earlier view of which is included above. There are substantial differences evident - the stream has been culverted - the windows are altered and the building seems to have been heightened. Behind the school is School Brow Farm.

# Anderton Hall

**Anderton Hall. 1907:** Anderton Hall stood on the banks of the Lower Rivington Reservoir and was built in 1867 for Charles Joseph Stonor Esq. It was variously known as Stonor's Anderton Hall and Anderton New Hall, the latter to distinguish it from Anderton Old Hall which was situated between Crown Lane, Horwich, and Anderton Lane, Anderton. Anderton New Hall comprised 47 rooms with a ballroom in the south wing. Local Catholics were allowed to use the Roman Catholic Chapel at the Hall until the building of St. Joseph's Church, Anderton in 1863. The last tenant was James Lawrence, a mill-owner, and following his departure in 1930 the property was demolished on the grounds that there was no demand at the time for such a property.

Close up views of Anderton Hall. c.1890.

Alderman James Lawrence,
the last tenant of Anderton Hall. c.1904.

The 'Anderton' Stone.
This interesting carved stone is preserved in Rivington Church
grounds and has been the subject of a great deal of debate as to
its origins. The name is derived from the emblem of the Anderton
family, the three shackbolts carved on the bottom right of the
stone.

# Beech House and Beech Cottage

**Beech House and Beech Cottage, Rivington. c.1910:** Beech House was originally built in the 18th century when it was known as Smith's House. In 1860, the Ainsworth family, bleachers of Bolton, had the property extended. It is thought that the property derived its name from the fact that the oldest known specimen of a beech tree stood nearby. The last tenant of the house was Richmond Leigh who left in 1919 after which the property was demolished. Beech Cottage still exists as a private residence.

View of Beech House (left) and Beech Cottage (right) with Rivington Pike in the background. c.1905.

This photograph shows the old beech tree from which the names of Beech House and Beech Cottage were derived. The tree was struck by lightning in the 1950's and had to be felled.

# Darbyshire's Cottage
# (Water Hey Cottage)

**Darbyshire's Cottage (also known as Water Hey Cot) c.1905:** Charles James Darbyshire who was the first Mayor of Bolton in 1838/39 resided at the cottage. He died on the 22nd June 1874 and is buried in Rivington Chapel graveyard.

Charles James Darbyshire. c.1865.

# Dean Wood House, Rivington

**Dean Wood House, Rivington. c.1900:** Dean Wood House was constructed with compensation monies awarded to the Smithills family following the construction of Rivington Reservoirs. On the death of Mr. Smithills in 1902, his widow did not wish to continue occupancy and the house was made the subject of compulsory purchase by the water authorities. The stone from which the property was built came from Turner's Farm, the site of which was submerged beneath the waters of Yarrow Reservoir.

George Nuttall Shawcross. M.B.E. George Nuttall Shawcross was born at Vauze House, Blackrod, in 1874. In 1881 the family moved to Rose Cottage, Rivington. and in 1927 to Dean Wood House. Mr. Shawcross worked at Horwich Locomotive Works and was General Manager from 1924 to 1936. In 1920 he was awarded the M.B.E. for keeping the Loco. Works Foundry operating during the First World War. He left the district in 1950 to live in Windsor where he died the following year. He was a keen historian responsible for a number of pamphlets on local history. The Shawcross family were descended from Lord Willoughby of Parham in Suffolk.

Mrs Sarah Ellen Shawcross (nee Salt) who was the mother of George Nuttall Shawcross.

# Knowle House, Rivington

*Above:* **Knowle House, Rivington. c.1905:** Mr. Arthur Middleton, a partner in Middleton's Springfield Mill, Heath Charnock, was instrumental in having Knowle House constructed in the 1870's. The distinctive building with its many gables is presently used as a private nursing home.

*Below:* Knowle House, Rivington. This view of Knowle House is taken from a post-card postally used on the 24th July 1906.

KNOWLE HOUSE RIVINGTON

# Red Cot

*Above:* **Red Cot, Rivington. c.1905:** Red Cot was built at the end of the 19th century for a spinster who wanted to move into the village to live. This interesting post-card photograph shows the property to the right with the distinctive outline of Rockhaven Castle on the skyline to the left.

*Below:* **Red Cot. c.1905:** A close up view of Red Cot which was also produced as a post-card. Mr. James Anderton who was the Chairman of Rivington Parish Council, lived at this address until his death and his widow still owns the property.

# Sheephouse Cottage

**Sheephouse Cottage, Sheephouse Lane, Rivington. 1942:** Sheephouse Cottage was situated where Hall Lane junctions with Sheephouse Lane. It may be that the name of the cottage derives from Sheephouse Farm which existed before the reservoirs were built. Harry Towler tenanted the cottage for many years and was a familiar and friendly figure. The photograph, taken in 1942, shows Mr. Towler at the gate of his home, in conversation.

# The 'Street', Rivington

**The 'Street', Rivington. c.1900:** There is a reference to Alexander Street owning an estate in Rivington during 1534. He had five daughters and following his death that year (1534) Richard Standish, a distant cousin, moved into the property to take possession of it on the premise that he was acting as guardian to the deceased's children. In the event, Richard Standish was shown to have no legal claim and was dispossessed of the 'Street'. A suitable guardian was then appointed by the courts. Peter Martin, who was born on the 5th May 1802, came into possession of the 'Street' on his marriage to Mary Tetley Walker. The original 'Street' was demolished in the early 1850's when the reservoirs were built and was replaced by compensation monies with the building shown above. It was this property that Peter Martin and his wife moved into in 1853. Peter Martin was a textile magnate who owned mills in Bolton and Farnworth. Among a number of generous benefactions he made were a donation towards the cost of extending Bolton Infirmary in 1841, and the building of Horwich Public Hall in 1878/1879 which was totally financed by him. Horwich Public Hall was officially opened on the 2nd April 1879, but sadly, Peter Martin only survived the ceremony for a short time - his death occurring on the 12th July 1879. In 1882 his widow presented the Hall for use by the township of Horwich. The 'Street' is at present in use as private accommodation having been divided into four luxury self-contained flats.

Close up view of the 'Street'. c.1900.

This view of the 'Street' looking across Upper Rivington Reservoir is dated c.1885.

# Summerfield, Rivington

**Summerfield, Rivington. c.1900:** Summerfield was built on the site of an old stone cottage known as 'Old Thatch'. It was once the home of Mr. R. G. Hinnel, who was Town Clerk of Bolton from 1865 to 1905. The house was subsequently demolished in the 1920's.

# Ward's Cottage and Ward Hill

**Ward's Cottage and Ward Hill, Rivington c.1900:** Ward's Cottage is to the right with Ward Hill, the taller property on the left. Ward's Farm was built in 1720 by Thomas Brownlow and included the property known as Ward's Cottage. Ward Hill was built in 1856 by Mr. William Ryder who was the founder of the Bee-Hive Spindle and Fly Works in Bolton.

**Rivington Pike from Anderton Hall. c.1880:** This unusual view of Rivington across the Lower Rivington Reservoir shows several properties including (on the right), Ward Hill; Ward's Cottage and Ward's Farm. This contradicts previous information that Ward's Cottage was built on the site of Ward's Farm.

# Ainsworth's Farm (Wood's Farm) Rivington

**Ainsworth's Farm or Woods Farm, Rivington. c.1910:** The farm was originally built by James Isherwood in 1698 and a commemorative datestone can be seen in Rivington Chapel graveyard, which was placed there following the demolition of the farm in the early years of this century. James Wood and Margaret Wood lived at the farm for many years. They were reported to be descendants of Executioner Whowell who carried out the execution of Lord Derby in Bolton.

Margaret Woods. (born 28th June 1835)

James Woods. (born 4th October 1840)

Close up view of Ainsworth (Wood's) Farm. c.1900.

# Ashworth's Farm or Middle Derbyshires

**Ashworth's Farm or Middle Derbyshires. c.1920:** Ashworth's Farm or Middle Derbyshires was re-built in 1857 just after the construction of the Rivington Reservoirs. At one time a part of the property was used as a pub which traded under the name of the Willoughby Arms, but was better known locally as Fanny's Cat - a nickname derived from the tenant - Fanny Crompton. There are two men visible to the left of the farm and the one standing on the right wearing a trilby has been identified as George Ashworth.

# Gorton Farm (Old Lord's)

**Gorton Farm (Old Lord's). c.1910:** Gorton Farm was once the home of Lord Willoughby and is also known as Old Lord's Farm. The ivy-covered farm is to the right with the barns and outbuilding close by. Old Will's Farm is standing just behind the farm buildings with Higher Knowle Farm just below and to the left of Rivington Pike Tower.

# Great House Farm, Rivington

**Great House Farm Rivington. c.1905: T**he Broadhurst family owned Great House Farm in the 13th century and it was subsequently occupied by the Bullough and Shaw families. The latter sold the farm to Thomas Anderton of Rivington in 1699. There is a record of John Norcross who was Master of Rivington Grammar School renting the property in 1767. Lord Leverhulme eventually came to own the property when he purchased Rivington Manor in 1900 but it passed to Liverpool Corporation by compulsory purchase in 1902.

Valuable Freehold Farms at Ashton-upon-Mersey, Cheshire, and Rivington, Lancashire.

TO BE SOLD BY AUCTION, by Messrs. WILLIAM WILSON and SON, at the Mitre Hotel, Manchester, on Tuesday, 10th October, 1893, at four for five o'clock in the evening, subject to conditions of sale:

Lot 1. A FREEHOLD FARMHOUSE known as Weathercock Hall, with the Farm Buildings and Fields adjoining, situate in Ashton-upon-Mersey, in the county of Chester, containing 13a. 0r. 30p. 7yds. or thereabouts.

Lot 2. A FREEHOLD CLOSE of Excellent GRASS LAND, situate in Ashton-upon-Mersey aforesaid, containing 6a. 0r. 24p. or thereabouts.

Lot 3. A FREEHOLD CLOSE of Excellent GRASS LAND adjoining the river Mersey, situate partly in Ashton-upon-Mersey aforesaid and partly in Urmston, in the county of Lancaster, containing 7a. 1r. 4p. 4yds. or thereabouts.

Lot 4. The FREEHOLD FARM known as Great House, with the Farm Buildings, Cottage, and Fields adjoining, situate in Rivington, in the county of Lancaster, containing 23a. 3r. 21p. or thereabouts.

The whole of the lots are free from chief rent. Lots 1, 2, and 3 are free from land tax and are subject to tithe rent charges amounting to £3. 14s. 9d. per annum, and lot 4 to tithe rent charges of £1. 12s. 6d. and a Duchy charge of 5d. per annum. Lots 1, 2, and 3 are in the occupation of Mr. Philip Potts, who has undertaken to give up possession on completion. Lot 4 is in the occupation of Mr. Robert Smith as yearly tenant at a rent of £40 per annum.—Plans and further particulars may be obtained of the Auctioneers, 29, Fountain-street, Manchester; Messrs. DENDY & PATERSON, 5, Cross-street, Manchester; or Messrs. Janson, Cobb, Pearson, and Co., solicitors, 41, Finsbury Circus, London, E.C.

Robert Smith who was the last farmer at Great House Farm, photographed in Adlington.

Great House Farm, Rivington. c.1898.

GREAT HOUSE FARM & PIKE RIVINGTON.

**Great House Barn. c.1890:** The barn is standing extreme left with the farm to the right. This barn was converted into a refreshment room by Lord Leverhulme and it is interesting to compare this view with the one showing the conversion.

Interior of Great House Barn. c.1898

# Higher Knowle Farm

Higher Knowle Farm. 1916: In the endowment deed for Rivington Grammar School dated the 6th September 1574, Bishop Pilkington is recorded as having undertaken the purchase of Higher Knowle, Lower Knowle and Grut Farms from Christopher Anderton. Over a century later in 1698, Thomas Entwistle of Higher Knowle was churchwarden at Rivington Church. John Shaw and his wife Sarah (nee Brownlow) were residents at Higher Knowle Farm from the 1740's and portraits of their daughters Esther, Mary and Anne still exist, copies of which are reproduced below. The portraits date from 1770. Little is known of Esther and Anne but Mary married John Salt, a Bolton solicitor.

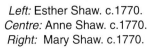

*Left:* Esther Shaw. c.1770.
*Centre:* Anne Shaw. c.1770.
*Right:* Mary Shaw. c.1770.

# Higher Ward's Farm
# (Clock House)

**Higher Ward's Farm, (Clock House), Rivington. c.1890:** On the 8th May 1569, Giles Ward of Rivington made agreement to construct Higher Ward's Farm for Leonard Pilkington and his sister, Alice. The farm was known locally as 'Clock House' a name which was adopted when the lady tenant used to leave the front door of the property open so that the scholars on their way to the Grammar School could see the time by the large grandfather clock situated just inside the doorway. The last tenants of the farm were the Lee family. In 1905 the farm was demolished.

**Higher Ward's Farm. c.1900:** Mrs Lee is standing to the right in a white apron. It seems to be washing day judging by the washing line behind the farm. The two youths near the fence are Arthur Hudson (left) and Thomas Hough.

# Intack Farm, Rivington

**Intack Farm, Rivington, c.1904:** This post-card view of Intack Farm was postally used on the 9th May 1904. The farm was re-built in 1712 by Richard Brownlow and extended by Mr. Entwistle about 1880. The property was finally demolished in 1908. One feature of the farm was a sunken garden.

Close up view of Intack Farm. c.1900.

# New Hall Farm

**New Hall Farm, Rivington. c.1900:** There is a record of Robert Pilkington giving his son, Richard, New Hall Farm as a wedding present in 1336. The property included a water corn mill and kiln. The above property was demolished early this century and even the barn which is all that remains, is in a state of dereliction.

This charming old photograph was reproduced from a glass negative in 1937 and dates from c.1890. Miss Sarah Howarth of New Hall Farm, Rivington, is seated to the right, with her cousin Mrs John Dickinson in the centre and Miss Esther Salt on the left.

**New Hall Farm Barn. 1990:** The stone effigy of a Moor's head taken from the original Black–A–Moor's Head Inn was built into the wall of New Hall Barn. Sadly the barn is presently in a state of dereliction the roof timbers having recently collapsed.

# Old Rachel's Farm

**Old Rachel's Farm. c.1880:** Mrs Evans is standing with arms akimbo outside her home.

# Pilkington's Farm

**Pilkington's Farm and the 'Street', Rivington. c.1905:** Pilkington's Farm is the building to the right with the farm's outbuildings on the left. The 'Street' can be seen in the background across the Upper Rivington Reservoir.

# Rivington Hall Farm

**Rivington Hall Farm. c.1905:** The terrace shown above contains two separate properties, Rivington Hall Farm and a cottage which is seen far right. The farm initially supported the manorial lord and was last operated by Peter Brownlow who worked for the Crompton family who lived at Rivington Hall until 1910. At present the property is private housing.

# School Brow Farm, Rivington

**School Brow Farm. c.1890:** In the original lease of the school-house to Robert Dewhurst schoolmaster of Rivington Grammar School drawn up in 1581, there is mention of School Brow Farm. James and Janet Anderton rented the farm in 1610 at an annual fee of 15s . 8d (78 new pence) in addition to which they had to provide six hens to the Lord of Rivington Manor at Christmas and complete six days reaping in the landlord's field during harvest without pay. The property was completely re-built by Thomas Anderton in 1695. The last tenants of School Brow Farm were the Southworth family who, following the demolition of the property in 1908, removed to Sweetlove's Farm.

View of School Brow Farm across the Lower Rivington Reservoir. Rivington Day School is visible extreme left. c.1910.

**Rivington viewed across Lower Rivington Reservoir from Anderton Hall. c.1880:** The ivy covered building in the centre background is School Brow Farm, and the Black - A - Moor's Head Inn can be seen on the left just below Rivington Church.

# Sweetlove's Farm

SWEETLOVES RIVINGTON.

**Sweetlove's Farm. c.1890:** Edmund Sweetlove who was Usher (Deputy Headmaster) at Rivington Grammar School from 1688 until 1733 had Sweetlove's Farm built in 1714. A datestone on the gable of the property reads 'S over E. A. G. - 1714'. In the will of Robert Anderton of Great House, dated 10th October 1716, Edmund Sweetlove and John Walker were left joint ownership of Great House and appointed executors in respect of a tenement in the Anderton District. In the severe winter of 1939/40 the snow was so deep in Rivington that on the death of Mr. Peachall, a retired school teacher, at Sweetlove's Farm his body had to be taken to Rivington Church for interment on a sled.

# Simm's Farm

**Simm's Farm. c.1890:** Simm's Farm stood on Rivington Lane quite close to Pall Mall Cottages but on the opposite side of the road. It was occupied in 1902 by Abraham Taylor and his family. Abraham's son, Roscoe Taylor, was the Chairman of Horwich Urban District Council in 1928/29.

# Top o'th Hill Farm

**Top o'th Hill Farm, 26th August 1961.** In 1841 John Nightingale farmed Top o'th Hill with the assistance of John and Elizabeth Turner whom he employed as an agricultural labourer and a servant, respectively. In addition, Mr Nightingale had responsibility for Charles Hornby, described as a 15 year old mental defective. It seems that Mr and Mrs Turner eventually took over the farm because they are recorded as being responsible for the property in 1851. The farm was re-built in 1898. The Makinson family lived at the farm from early this century and the holding is also known as Makinson's Farm.

# Cottages

*Above:* **Mill Hill Cottages. 1933:** Mill Hill Cottages were built by John Hampson in 1788. They were originally intended for occupation by weavers.

*Below:* **Pall Mall Cottages. 1921:** The first cottage on the right was once the home of the policeman who was responsible for law and order in Lever Park. Beech Cottage is to the left.

**Rose Cottages c.1910:** When Liverpool Corporation were granted rights of compulsory purchase in Rivington, Mr Walton Ainsworth of Beech House received £11,000 for his estate which included Beech House and outbuildings, Beech Cottage, Rose Cottages and Middle Derbyshires with 21 acres of land. At least one other property in Rivington bore the name Rose Cottage, which causes confusion. However the Rose Cottages sold as above were also known as ~Top o'th Meadows. They no longer exist.

# William Hesketh Lever
# (later Lord Leverhulme)

William Hesketh Lever, later Lord Leverhulme, was born at 6 Wood Street, Bolton, on the 19th September 1851. His parents ran a thriving wholesale grocery business in Bank Street, Bolton, and Lord Leverhulme was the eldest of two sons in a family of ten children.

Rivington was a popular beauty spot from which to escape the atmosphere of an industrial town and the young William formed a great attachment to the area.

Following an extremely successful business life which saw the construction of Port Sunlight where the world famous 'Sunlight' soap was manufactured, Lord Leverhulme purchased Rivington Manor from the Crompton family in 1900.

There was a particular spot on the moorland above Rivington where Lord Leverhulme spent many hours during his courtship with Elizabeth Ellen Hulme who was to become his wife. Instead of living in Rivington Hall, which was the manorial seat, Lord Leverhulme had a sectional wooden bungalow erected on the 1000 foot contour of Rivington Moor near to the favourite spot of his courtship days.

Right up to the time of his death on 7th May 1925, Lord Leverhulme was involved in setting up Rivington as a tourist attraction. He spent a fortune on the construction of Lever Park and improved the roadways and amenities of the area. In September 1901 he made a gift of Lever Park to the people of Bolton and the surrounding district which was gratefully accepted. He retained the 45 acre 'Bungalow' site for his own use.

Liverpool Corporation were concerned at the development taking place in Rivington because there was potential for pollution of the water supply and promoted a Bill before Parliament which eventually entitled them to obtain the lands owned by Lord Leverhulme, with the exception of the Bungalow grounds, by compulsory purchase. Nevertheless, the plans for Lever Park went ahead. Rivington Hall was set up as a museum and two barns, one belonging to Rivington Hall Farm and one to Great House Farm, were converted for use as refreshment rooms. Lever Park was stocked with a variety of wild animals and the roadways were greatly improved to facilitate access.

The Bungalow Grounds remained private except on the occasional 'open days' when a small charge was levied to visit them and the monies were donated to charity.

In 1913 the first sectional wooden bungalow was razed to the ground by Edith Rigby, a militant Suffragette from Preston, who was trying to draw attention to the cause she so fervently supported. A second bungalow was built of stone and stood until 1947 when it was eventually demolished.

Much of Lord Leverhulme's gift remains for the public to enjoy and Rivington is fortunate that such a generous benefactor favoured the area with his attention.

William Hesketh Lever (Lord Leverhulme) accepted the Mayoralty of Bolton in 1918. His wife's death in 1913 meant that the position of Mayoress was filled by his daughter-in-law.

Coat-of-Arms of Lord Leverhulme who bought Rivington Manor in 1900 from the Crompton family. The motto 'Mutare vel timere sperno' translates as 'To change or to fear I spurn'.

# Rivington Bungalow
# (Roynton Cottage)

The first Rivington Bungalow built by Lord Leverhulme on the 1000 foot contour of Rivington Moor was a section wooden 'shooting box' supplied by the Portable Building Company of 46a Market Street, Manchester.

The first Rivington Bungalow (Roynton Cottage) c.1900.

Roynton Cottage. c.1905.

**Roynton Cottage. c.1910:** Lord Leverhulme had the original sectional wooden building improved and extended out of all recognition. This photograph shows some of the alterations effected.

THE BUNGALOW, RIVINGTON.                    Nº 3.A.

**Roynton Cottage.** The moorland surrounding the bungalow was transformed into beautiful garden areas. This view shows a gardener at work on the north front. The grassed area in the centre was used as a bowling green.

# Arson Attack on the First Bungalow
# (Roynton Cottage)

On Monday 7th July 1913, Mrs. Edith Rigby, a militant suffragette who lived in Winckley Square, Preston, carried out an arson attack on Roynton Cottage. She had travelled to Rivington in her husband's car driven by the family chauffeur and was also accompanied by Albert Yeadon. Cans of paraffin were taken up to the bungalow site by Mrs Rigby and Albert Yeadon, but she then asked Mr. Yeadon to leave so that she could execute her plan personally. There was no one in residence at the bungalow so it was an easy matter to break windows and spread the paraffin to maximise the amount of damage. When ignited, the timber structure quickly spread the fire and the whole building was razed to the ground.

Rivington Pike Tower can be seen extreme right on this shot of the burned out bungalow.

# The Second Bungalow

Following the arson attack on Roynton Cottage, Lord Leverhulme quickly had plans drawn up for a second bungalow, but this one was to be constructed of stone to avoid such catastrophic losses. A veritable fortune in works of art had been destroyed in the fire at Roynton Cottage.

A second building known simply as The Bungalow was built and ready for occupation less than one year after the fire.

**The Bungalow, Rivington. c.1920:** The circle above the porchway includes the date of construction - 1914.

**The Bungalow, Rivington,. c.1925:** A ballroom was built at the property in 1923 on the site of what was once a garth or walled garden. The pigeon tower from inside the garth was moved to the front on the Bungalow and assists in establishing the date.

The Garth (walled garden) at The Bungalow. c.1920.

View of the front of The Bungalow from the driveway. The stones on the left were intended for the construction of a rockery about 1930.

# Lodge Houses to the Bungalow

The Bungalow and grounds were essentially private property and a lodge house was situated at each of the four entrance points occupied by staff of Lord Leverhulme. The lodges were known as Bolton Lodge; Belmont Lodge; South Lodge and Stone House Lodge. These interesting individually designed properties, provided comfortable accommodation for staff members.

## Bolton Lodge

Bolton Lodge was situated at the entrance to the Bungalow grounds from George's Lane. It was originally a thatched house but the thatch was replaced by tiles.

**Bolton Lodge. c.1905:** The thatched roof of Bolton Lodge can be seen with Rivington Pike in the background.

THE PIKE, RIVINGTON, FROM BUNGALOW.    NO. 9, COPYRIGHT.

**Bolton Lodge. c.1920:** In this post-card view the thatched roof of Bolton Lodge has been replaced by tiles.

# Stone House Lodge

**Stone House Lodge. c.1920:** This unusual property straddled the driveway into the Bungalow grounds. At one time in was occupied by the Shone family. Mr. Shone was the Estate Factor mainly responsible for the gardens.

# South Lodge

**South Lodge. c.1930:** Situated at the lowest point of the grounds, South Lodge was a timbered structure with a thatched roof. Apparently this was the only property among the four lodge houses not equipped with electricity. It is nevertheless remembered as a comfortable house. The Storey family who were the last tenants before it was demolished had a particular affection for the place.

# Belmont Lodge

**Belmont Lodge. c.1907:** Belmont Lodge was also thatched and was sited at the entrance afforded from the direction of Belmont village. The first Bungalow is visible in the background. The visitors on this occasion were personal acquaintances of Lord Leverhulme.

# The Bungalow Grounds

The Bungalow grounds extended over 45 acres and it is not practicable other than to include a small selection of views of the beautiful gardens constructed by Lord Leverhulme. Neverthless, the attention to detail afforded and the fact that the gardens were constructed in a most unlikely spot where the top soil was extremely shallow with underlying rock gives some idea of the problems encountered in the design of these gardens.

View across Lower Rivington Reservoir from the Bungalow grounds. c.1920.

**Bungalow Grounds. c.1920.** The large rock seen right of centre, was left to show how much stone had to be excavated for the construction of the lawned area.

**Lord Leverhulme's Arched Bridge. c.1920:** The distinctive arched bridge pictured gave access to the Bungalow Grounds. Substantial metal railings were intended to keep out trespassers.

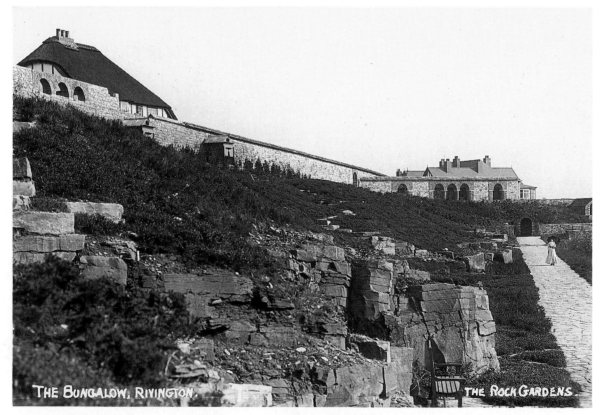

**The Rock Gardens. c.1907:** An excellent view of the rock gardens taken during the time of the first Bungalow. The Bungalow is to the right with Belmont Lodge House on the left.

*Above:* **Bungalow Grounds. c.1920:** The Pigeon Tower is to the right with loggia and summerhouses on the terraced gardens. Lord Leverhulme often went for a swim in the lake shown and at other times it was used for boating.

*Below:* **Bungalow Grounds. c.1920:** The summerhouse shown was one of several dispersed throughout the grounds. Each was equipped with seating on the inside and also on top of the roof.

**Boy and Dolphins. c.1920:** This fine statue stood in a small pool created by a waterfall. The distinctive plinth can still be seen in the grounds.

**Japanese Gardens, Rivington. c.1920:** The difficult problems encountered in construction are evident in these gardens built after the Japanese style.

# Bungalow Grounds Open Days

In the summer of 1911 Lord Leverhulme threw open his grounds to visitors on payment of a nominal fee which was donated to charity. Nearly 4,000 people visited the grounds on this occasion benefiting local charities to the amount of £77 .4s. 5d. The event proved so successful that it was repeated in subsequent years.

Visitors in the Bungalow Grounds. c.1920.

This group photograph of visitors to the Bungalow grounds was taken at one of the summerhouses - probably the one next to the great lawn. The style of dress suggests a date around 1910.

# Lever Park

At the entrance to Lever Park stand two granite pillars erected by the second Viscount Leverhulme in memory of his father who gave the park to the people of Bolton and the surrounding district. The pillars are inscribed as follows:-

(Left Hand Pillar) - 'LEVER PARK - THE GIFT OF WILLIAM HESKETH LEVER - 1st VISCOUNT LEVERHULME - BORN AT 6 WOOD STREET, BOLTON SEPTEMBER 19th 1851. DIED AT HAMPSTEAD, LONDON. MAY 7TH 1925. - FOR THE BENEFIT OF THE CITIZENS OF HIS NATIVE TOWN AND NEIGHBOURHOOD BY ACT OF PARLIAMENT IN 1902 THE OWNERSHIP AND CARE OF THE PARK WERE VESTED IN THE CORPORATION OF THE CITY OF LIVERPOOL.'

(Right hand pillar) - 'LEVER PARK - THESE PYLONS WERE ERECTED BY WILLIAM HULME 2nd VISCOUNT LEVERHULME TO COMMEMORATE THE GIFT OF LEVER PARK BY HIS FATHER 1934.'

Lever Park with Rivington and Blackrod Grammar School visible on the left. At the time that this photograph was taken Lever Park Avenue had not been built.

**View across Lever Park taken from old Horwich Racecourse. c.1905:** Gorton Farm (Old Lord's); Old Will's Farm and Higher Knowle Farm can be seen to the right with Knowle House chimneys and gables visible to the left.

**Lever Park and the Bungalow Grounds. c.1920:** South Lodge stands bottom left with the Pigeon Tower above it and Belmont Lodge in the centre. The second Bungalow is on the skyline extreme right.

This view across the Lower Rivington Reservoir is taken from a post-card, postally used on 24th June 1923. The reverse contains the message, 'This is the view from my bedroom window only it is further away'. Anderton Hall and its outbuildings can be seen on the opposite side of the Lower Rivington Reservoir, far left.

Lever Park from the Bungalow grounds. c.1913.

# Lever Park 'Zoo'

John Mulligan of Rivington Hall with a lion cub. c.1920.

Stags in Lever Park. c.1910.

Zebras grazing in Lever Park. c.1910.

# Rivington Barns

Rivington Hall Barn. c.1910. Lord Leverhulme had Rivington Hall Barn and Great House Barn converted into refreshment rooms to accommodate visitors to Lever Park.

Interior of Rivington Hall Barn. c.1910.

Rear of Rivington Hall Barn. c.1905.

**Great House Barn. c.1930:** The Mulligan family held the franchise from Lord Leverhulme to provide refreshments at the two barns from 1902. The family lived at Rivington Hall. Mrs Ethel Coupe (nee Mulligan) can be seen in the photograph serving tea at Great House Barn.

## Lever Park Refreshment Rooms
## Rivington

| | | |
|---|---|---|
| Pot of Tea, Bread & Butter | .................... | 8d |
| ,, | Jam .................... | 11 |
| ,, | Boiled Egg.............. | 1 - 0 |
| ,, | Fruit Salad ......... | 1 - 3 |
| ,, | Pears, Peaches or Apricots ....... | 1 - 2 |
| | (Cream 3d. extra) | |
| ,, | Green Salad ......... | 1 - 2 |
| ,, | Salmon (tinned) ...... | 1 - 4 |
| ,, | Sardines ,, ....... | 1 - 2 |
| ,, | Crab ,, ....... | 1 - 8 |
| ,, | Lobster ,, ....... | 1 - 10 |
| ,, | Boiled Ham ........ | 1 - 6 |
| ,, ,, ,, | Cold Beef ............ | 1 - 6 |
| ,, ,, ,, | Tongue ............... | 1 - 8 |

Buttered Scones 2d.     Chocolate Biscuits 2d.

Cakes 2d.     Assorted Biscuits.

**PARTIES CATERED FOR**

T. N. GARSTANG, PRINTER, HORWICH

**Menu card for Rivington Barns signed by Gracie Fields. c.1934:** Several famous names have lunched at the Barns over the years including the Indian leader, Ghandi, and Gracie Fields, the Lancashire songstress. On her visit to the Barns about 1934 'Our Gracie' signed the menu card.

**Great House Barn. c.1910:** A comparison with the earlier photograph included of Great House Farm and Barn shows the amount of alteration which was effected to convert the structure into a refreshment room. At the time of writing (1995) the roof of this barn is undergoing substantial renovation and it seems that the stone roofing tiles will need to be replaced.

GREAT HOUSE BARN, RIVINGTON.

The two photographs below show the present day renovation taking place at Great house barn.

# The Clog Inn, Anglezarke

**The Clog Inn, Anglezarke. c.1900:** John Wilson was responsible for the erection of the Clog Inn in 1710. The premises saw an upturn in business while the reservoirs were being constructed in the 1850's. The pub was used as a base for the workmen during this period.

**The Clog Inn, Anglezarke. c.1920:** This post-card view of the Clog Inn was taken by H. G. Hutchinson and shows the building in a state of dereliction. There is no glass in the windows and the roof tiles are missing from the building on the right.

**The Clog Inn, Anglezarke, c.1880:** As can be seen from this early photograph the Clog Inn comprised a complex of buildings. The shafts of several carts can be seen on the left.

**The Clog Inn, Anglezarke, c.1880:** The datestone visible behind the rider reads I.W. 1710 and refers to John Wilson who built the premises in 1710. (An 'I' was used for a 'J' when carving).

**The Clog Inn, c.1880:** A close-up view of the premises.

**The Clog Inn, c.1880:** This interesting view shows one of the outbuildings of the Clog Inn complex with Leicester (or Lester) Mill Quarry in the background. The gantry (top right) suggests that the quarry was being worked at the time.

# Yew Tree Inn, Heath Charnock

**Berry's Yew Tree Inn. c.1880:** Dill Cottage was converted into licensed premises by John Berry. The pub was known locally as the 'Frozen Mop'.

# Anglezarke

**Rivington Reservoirs. c.1880:** This view of the Anglezarke Reservoir and the Upper and Lower Rivington Reservoirs is contained in a famous painting by Frederick William Hulme (1816 - 1884) and is exhibited in Bolton Museum. The 'Street' can be seen on the extreme centre right of the photograph.

**High Bullough (Chorley) Reservoir, Anglezarke. c.1880:** Chorley Waterworks Company was the first to construct a reservoir in Anglezarke in 1850. The reservoir was relatively small covering 9 acres of Anglezarke Moor to a depth of 39 feet. The responsibilty for this reservoir was eventually taken over by the Liverpool Corporation Waterworks Company with the condition that they continued to supply water to the township of Chorley.

**Waterman's Cottage, Anglezarke. c.1880:** This picturesque mock Tudor house was built by Liverpool Corporation Waterworks Company for their resident engineer.

**Jacob's Ladder, Anglezarke c.1870:** A stairway used by the resident water engineer to gain access from Manor House to the Anglezarke Reservoir was known as Jacob's Ladder. It was only used for a short time and quickly fell into disrepair.

# EXTRACT FROM THE HORWICH POST OFFICE DIRECTORY FOR 1890

## RIVINGTON

RIVINGTON is a chapelry in the parish of Bolton, and in the union and postal district of Chorley. The incumbent of the Church is elected by the parishioners, and the living is at present filled by the Rev. W. Ritson, B.A. There is also a Unitarian Chapel in the vicinity. There is a Grammar School, founded by Bishop Pilkington in 1556, with which has been incorporated Blackrod Grammar School. This handsome building is partially endowed, and is under the mastership of the Rev. Geo. Squire, M.A. On the site of the old grammar school there is a day school. A charity is attached to Rivington, being left by the late Messrs. John and George Shaw to the industrious poor of Rivington and neighbourhood. The population in 1881 was 330. Acreage 2,767.

### PUBLIC INFORMATION

*Places of Worship and Schools*—Parish Church, Rev. W. Ritson, B.A., vicar. Unitarian Chapel, Rev. S. Thompson, minister. *Schools*—Rivington Elementary School ; Wm. Aulsebrook, master. Royal Grammar School, Rivington lane ; Rev. Geo. Squire, M.A., headmaster.

*Post Office*—Mrs. Jane Wilding, post-mistress. Nearest Telegraph & Money Order Office, at Horwich.

*Railway Stations*—Nearest stations at Horwich and Adlington.

*Resident Magistrates*—Walton Ainsworth, Esq., and J. W. Crompton, Esq.

### ALPHABETICAL DIRECTORY

Ainsworth Walton, cotton spinner (W. & C. Ainsworth), Beech house
Ashworth George, farmer, Higher Darbishires
Aulsebrook Wm., schoolmaster, Schoolhouses
Bain Jonathan, farmer, Great house
Berry Francis, farmer, Old Moses's
Berry John, farmer, Pilkingtons
Berry John, sexton, Mill hill
Bourne William, policeman, Pall mall
Brogden Joshua, carpenter, Prospect
Brownlow Christopher, sen., farmer, Old Rachels
Brownlow Christopher, jun., farmer, Brownhill
Brownlow Peter, farmer, Jepsons
Charlton Percival R., superintendent of filter beds, Lake cottage
Crompton John W., Rivington hall
Cunliffe George, farmer, Old Wills
Dixon Mrs. Emma M., Spring cottage
Entwistle Ralph, farmer, Lowerhouse
Fletcher Mrs. Mary A., Rivington hall
Foster Thomas, farmer, Wilcox
Gerrard Mrs. Ann, publican, Blackamoor's Head
Herbert Daniel, farmer, Grutt
Howarth John, farmer & assistant overseer, New hall
Hutchinson Thomas, farmer, Crosses, & carrier to Bolton
Johnson James, coal merchant, Summerfield
Lee James, farmer, Ellers
Lee Miss, Wardhill
Morris John, farmer, Hall dairy
Morris Mrs. Rachel, farmer, Intack
Parish Church and Schools ; Rev. W. Ritson, B.A., vicar ; Day school, Wm. Aulsebrook, master
Ritson Rev. William, B.A., The Parsonage
Rivington & Blackrod Grammar School, Rivington lane ; Rev. G. Squire, M.A., principal
Shaw Richard, Gillsbrook
Shawcross Mrs. Sarah Ellen, Rose cottage
Smith Edward, foreman of filter beds, Rivington lane
Squire Rev. G., M.A., head master, Grammar School
Taylor Abraham, farmer, Simms
Taylor John, farmer, Morris house
Taylor William, farmer, Green's farm
Thompson Rev. Samuel (Unitarian), Chape house
Thornley Samuel, gamekeeper, Kay's cottage
Unitarian Chapel ; Rev. S. Thompson, minister
Walsh Mrs. Ann, farmer, Old George's farm
Warburton The Misses, Lakeland Villas, Rivington lane
Wilding Mrs. Jane, shopkeeper (Post Office), School houses
Woods Charles, farmer, Ainsworths
Woods James, farmer, Ainsworths
Woods William, Old Kates

## ANGLEZARKE

ANGLEZARKE is a township and ancient parish of Bolton, from which town it is 8 miles distant, and from Chorley 2½ miles. The population in 1881 was 99. Acreage 2,570.

Nearest Post-office and Railway Station at Adlington.

Ashton William, mill manager, White coppice
Bellamy William, coachman, White coppice
Bithell Thomas, joiner, White coppice
Blackmore Wm. J. H., farmer, Jepsons
Catterall John, quarry owner, Leicester Mill ; res. Chorley
Catterall Mrs. Mary, beerseller, Lee Arms
Catterall Ralph, quarry manager, Lee house
Cousland John, waterman, Water house
Eccles Alfred E., cotton manufacturer, White Coppice Mill ; res. Albion villa
Fisher Daniel, farmer, Foggs
Halliwell Samuel, farmer, Bulloughs
Holt Chas., farmer, Brook house
Hope James T., weaver, White coppice
Smith John, butcher and stores manager, White coppice farm
Smith Joseph, farmer, White coppice
Smith William T., farmer, Snapes
White Coppice Co-operative Society, Limited, grocers and general dealers, the Wood ; Ernest Ashton, secretary ; John Smith, manager
Winstanley John, farmer, Garnett
Winstanley Roger, farmer, Siddow fold

---

# MEMORIÆ SACRVM

HERE LYETH BVRYED, THE BODY OF IOHN SHAWE, SECONDE SONNE OF LAWRENCE SHAWE OF HIGH BVLHAVGH IN ANLEYZARGH IN THE COVNTY OF LANC: BY WHOSE GVIFT & PROVISION OVT OF LANDES THE YEARLY SVMME OF TEN SHILLINGES IS TO BE PAYDE YEARLY FOR EVER, TOWARDS THE REPAYRE OF THIS CHVRCH OF RYVINGTON & ALSO THE YEARLY SVMME OF TWENTY NOBLES, TO BE DISTRIBVTED YEARLY FOR EVER, VNTO THE POORE PEOPLE INHABITING IN RYVINGTON ANLEYZARGH HEATH : CHERNOCKE AND ANDERTON IN THE SAYD COVNTY THE ONE MOYTIE ON GOOD FRAYDAY AND THE OTHER MOYTIE ON THE FIRST SONDAY IN ADVENT. HE DYED Yᵉ XII DAY OF NOVEMBER Aᵒ. DVI. 1627 BEING THEN OF Yᵉ AGE OF 55 YEARES

REVEL. 14.13. BLESSED ARE THE DEAD THAT DYE IN THE LORD EVEN SOE SAYTH THE SPIRITE FOR THEY REST FROM THEIR LABOVRS AND THEIR WORKES FOLLOWE THEM

AS I AM THOV SHALL BE.

A reminder of human mortality is contained in this brass memorial to John Shaw which is on the wall of Rivington Church.

# Miscellany

**Rivington Pike from Blackrod, 1834:** This drawing by G. Pickering was engraved by A.Le.Petit and appears in John Roby's 'Traditions of Lancashire'.

**Black-A-Moor's Head Inn. 1843:** This copy of a painting is held by the Crompton family and shows the annual donkey race passing the inn. The building was demolished when the reservoirs were built in the 1850's and a replacement was built with compensation monies near to Rivington Church.

**Lever Park Avenue, July 1936:** This photograph of the entrance to Lever Park Avenue from Scholes Bank, Horwich, was taken shortly after the two commemorative pillars were erected to Viscount Leverhulme.